Warren Holden

Autobiography of Love

Warren Holden

Autobiography of Love

ISBN/EAN: 9783337028954

Printed in Europe, USA, Canada, Australia, Japan

Cover: Foto ©Thomas Meinert / pixelio.de

More available books at **www.hansebooks.com**

PRESS OF J. B. LIPPINCOTT COMPANY

1888.

CONTENTS.

CONTENTS.

AUTOBIOGRAPHY OF LOVE.

AVANT-PROPOS.

CONSTANCY (1828).

How often hath the simple tale been told
  Of sudden, rapt, unutterable joy
  When love first thrills the heart of guileless
    boy,
And colors everything with rose and gold.
Once kindled, love's strong flame can ne'er grow
    cold ;
  The clouds of care may hide, but not destroy ;
  Nor will its honeyed sweetness ever cloy,
Though taste be delicate and culture old.
And even in the blissful realms above
  If aught could chill pure love's perennial glow,
    Let void Nirvana quench the conscious me.
Not Heaven shall make man false to boyhood's
    love.
  Embarked upon its tide shall being flow
    On in eternal continuity.

II.

ONE SPIRIT, MANY MANIFESTATIONS.

A CYNOSURE in boyhood's roseate sky,
  Her fairy figure floated airily
  To lure him onward towards his destiny,—
The heaven reflected in her laughing eye.
The altar where she prayed oft heard his sigh,
  For there betimes he bent the pious knee
  To worship God—in virgin purity.
'Twas bliss to be, if only she were nigh.
But each horizon brings bright stars to view;
  And many marvels love's career befall,
    Ere it may choose for better or for worse.
One substance many forms may well endue.
  Who shares the gift of God is heir to all
    The love whose beauty fills the universe.

YOUNG LOVE'S FIRST LAY.

Oh, my life, may our love, as with angels above,
  Never ebb, but flow onward for aye!
For better or worse, 'mid success or reverse,
  Be we tender and constant as they.

And still will I love thee wherever I rove,
  O'er the mountain or billowy main;
In sickness or health, or in want or in wealth,
  As I love thee, oh, love me again!

In the heat and the strife of an ever-vexed life
    With ambition let other hearts burn;
Full contented with this, we'll not ask other bliss
    Than to love and be loved in return.

Oh, tell of it not how in yonder lone spot,
    Where the evergreens fondly entwine,
Hand in hand we did plight, heart with heart to
    unite,—
    Yours the blessing, the blessèd was mine!

Then we pledged with love's seal that for woe
    or for weal
    The exchange should endure to the last,
And as oft as we sealed, each impression revealed
    Our engagement more full and more fast.

Like the flowers that blow where the lone waters
    flow,
  Unplucked by the thoughtless and gay,
We will hide our young love only witnessed
    above
  By the stars in their silent array;

We will seek a lone dell where in peace we may
    dwell,
  From the heartless and worldly removed,
Unpretending in worth, but with innocent mirth,
  Simply loving and being beloved.

INTERLUDE.

THE brooklet babbles by the way,
 The bird replies above.
And what, I pray you, may they say?
 The tale they tell is love.

LONGING.

As the constant dove bewaileth its love
  When absent from its side,
So for thee I pine, thou desire of mine,
  My own, my chosen bride.

In the silent night, when dreams of delight
  My waking fancies lull,
Then thou art there, oh, thou vision fair,
  "My own, my beautiful!"

Among the crowd of beauty proud
   One face alone I see;
And that sweet face, whence beams each grace,
   Belongeth to none but thee.

Reft part of my soul, to restore it whole,
   Thou must be my wedded wife;
Oh, haste the glad day,—I can brook no delay,—
   My love, my very life!

THE VESTAL VIRGIN.

SWEET virgin, priestess of my soul,
  My bosom is thy shrine;
I own thy mystical control,
  I'm all and only thine.

Here on the altar of my heart
  Thou fann'st the sacred flame,
And well dost act thy sisters' part
  Of yore, who did the same.

Pure vestal, in thy virgin pride,
   Fulfil thy pious vow;
Then will I claim thee for my bride.
   Oh, that the time were now!

VII.

INTERLUDE.

WELCOME, joyous spring,
  Bringing flowers.
Music birds are on the wing,
  Singing in thy bowers.
Happy love's the song they sing
  All the sunny hours.

2*

ABSENCE.

My heart is with thee, dearest,
  Though I wander far away;
And thine image still is nearest
  When loneliest I stray.

Doth not thy spirit hover,
  With tender sympathy,
O'er thy fond, faithful lover
  Who longs and weeps for thee?

Though envious space may sever
    Our bodies here below,
Our souls shall mingle ever
    In the land to which we go.

REPEAT THE TALE.

Oh, tell the rapturous story o'er
  Of how you learned to love me first,
And tell it as you told before
  When forth the glowing secret burst,
All eloquent with love-taught lore,
  With love-taught falterings interspersed!

Again my bounding heart shall beat
  While whispering sighs confess thee mine,
Again the willing vow repeat
  To be forever only thine;
And hope and memory be replete
  With dreams and visions all divine.

A gladness like they feel above
  Rushed through my heart and thrilled my frame,
When first, with accents of the dove,
  You called me by my household name,
As breathing from your lips of love
  My own dear William softly came.

Embarked on nature's happy tide,
  Oh, might the voyage of life be proved
With thee, dear Mary, by my side.
  We'd meet each adverse gale unmoved,
Rehearsing with alternate pride
  How well we love and are beloved.

Beloved by thee, to thee alone
  My heart's dear troth is ever due;
The faith of love then let us own,
  To all true bosoms always true.
My lady love, my only throne,
  My sweetheart, tell the tale anew.

OPPOSITION.

THEY told her she was cruelly deceived,
  A faithless lover had abandoned her.
But though her tender heart is deeply grieved,
  Yet quiet patience waits without demur.

Prophetic love hath visions of its own :
  She sees her lover fight his inward foe;
She hears with sympathy his piteous moan;
  She feels the anguish none but she may know.

The smiles and raillery of heartless wit,
  Like pointless arrows 'gainst a coat of mail,
Fall harmless at her feet, or never hit.
  By her own heart she knows he cannot fail.

Fidelity, oh, thou art wondrous strong!
  Nor time, nor death thy constancy decrease.
To thee the endless eons shall belong,
  With tranquil days of sweet, unruffled peace.

XI.

WOMELSDORF.

Dear old Womelsdorf,
  Quaint and quiet town;
Hospitable wharf
  When love was like to drown.

Pennsylvania Dutch
  Was the common speech;
Though I listened much,
  Quite beyond my reach.

But one voice I heard
  Would be understood,
Though no single word
  Smacked of Saxon good.

That was love's sweet voice,
  Recognized by tone;
Interpreted by choice
  Or by gesture known.

Love not garrulous
  Pleads in silent look,
Proxy speaks for us
  Through the babbling brook.

Sweetly singing birds
  Tell the tender tale.
Love can hear its words
  Whispered by the gale.

Womelsdorf, of old,
  What thou wast to me
Tongue hath never told:
  Love alone could see.

XII.

JEALOUSY.

So you sought her in my exile,
   Thought to win the pearl of price,
Hoped to find her weak and flexile,
   Tried the trick of loaded dice.

Did you think the senseless clamor,
   Of her lover proved untrue,
Could induce a magic glamour
   That would see a saint in you?

Did you deem the soul of honor
   Could be bought as cheap as dirt;
That you could prevail upon her
   Easy as on fickle flirt?

Paltry object of derision,
  Woe-begone, you turned to go,
When, with mild but firm decision,
  Instantly she answered no!

Blasted be the mean ambition
  That could steal a broken heart;
May it find its just perdition,
  Victim of its own vile art.

SYMPATHY OF NATURE.

FRIENDLY trees, familiar grass,
Saw you not my lady pass,
Crowned with wreath of golden hair,
Brighter than the locks you wear?
When again she walks this way
Note her elegant array;
How she moves with courtly pace,
Belle of beauty, queen of grace.

Warbling love lays, pretty bird,
Sure I am you must have heard.
Eyes she has of heavenly blue,
And she carols sweet as you.

Streamlet, purling as you flow,
You, too, seem my love to know.
Tell it not, thou babbling brook,
How in yonder shady nook
Where the loving tendrils twine
Twice she promised to be mine.

River, rushing to the sea,
We will come and sail with thee,—
Steer our bark to lonely isle,
Far aloof from wicked wile;
Placid life shall glide away,
Dreaming, dreaming, day by day.

XIV.

LOVE'S EXILE.

RETURN, return, my banished lover;
  Stricken heart, no longer stray.
Oh, let my yearning breast recover
  All the peace you took away!

Come back, come back, I'm lone and weary,
  Longing, waiting, day by day;
Waking through the midnight eerie,
  I can only watch and pray.

Forgive, forgive, my heart is breaking.
  Come, oh, come, thou hast the balm,—
The only balm to soothe its aching,
  Bringing back my wonted calm!

Thou canst not come? Then I must follow,
  Though I brave the cruel sea.
The heartless world is false and hollow:
  Better, far, is death with thee.

THE QUEST OF LOVE.

OH, holy love, where dwellest thou?
A pilgrim, urged by pious vow,
Devoted at thy shrine would bow
    And lay a heart of truth.
Guide me to thy enchanted mount,
And bathe me in that living fount
Which blots remorseless Time's account
    And gives immortal youth;

Impart the secret cipher key
To unlock the sacred mystery,
And read from book of destiny
  The riddle of my life.
Gifted with poet's second-sight,
And led by fancy's magic light,
Must I pursue the visions bright
  Wherewith thy realm is rife?

On nature's mother lap recline,
And, gazing in her face, divine
The traits that multiform combine
  In harmonies unknown?
Or dig the inestimable ore
From mines of philosophic lore,
Which ancient sages bade explore
  To win the alchemic stone?

Enshrined in purest maiden breast,
Fit temple for the heavenly guest,
There, say, hast thou set up thy rest
   And bid thy votaries come?
Or else in friendship's warm embrace,
Or fellow-feeling for our race,
In patriot zeal or hermit grace
   Is thy congenial home?

Each source my trusting spirit tries;
Each specious hope exhausted lies,
A group of blighted vanities,
   "In Disappointment's grave."
Like bubbles dancing down the stream
Freighted with rainbow hues that gleam
A moment in the sun's bright beam,
   Then burst upon the wave.

Hast thou no place of peaceful rest,
But wanderest from breast to breast,
An angel visitant at best
　　That mockest young desire?
A weary pilgrimage was mine,
Oft dreaming I had found thy shrine
Where *ignis fatuus* chanced to shine,
　　No constant altar's fire.

And still for love my bosom sighed;
Nor was my prayer at last denied:
A small, still voice within replied
　　In dictates from above,—
" Be duty's thorny pathway trod,
Nor shun the cross, nor fear the rod;
Love pleasure not, love only God,
　　For God alone is love."

ODE TO LOVE.

A WORD of nature's coinage,—love.
   She never struck a truer.
The silvery sound alone will prove
   The metal to be pure.
A sympathetic thrill it starts,
Which makes it current with young hearts
   When uttered by a wooer.

Was human passion ever seen
  In fitter garments dressed?
Soft, flowing, modest, and serene,
Like nature's robe of living green
  That soothes the tender eye the best,
  Its gentle cadence soothes the breast.

Love wields mysterious power.
  The few who know its quiet use
    Achieve momentous victories.
Weak woman makes it her strong tower
  Whence she displays the flag of truce,
    Her constant watchword peace.

Her wont is thither to retreat
  When clouds of sorrow hover o'er;
There safest refuge doth she meet
When man's fierce passions in their heat
  On her devoted head would pour,
  Though the sin lieth at his door.

Thou better angel of the soul,
  Mild umpire of the passions,
  To shame their wayward fashions;
When, subject to thy just control,
  Intestine quarrels cease,
  How brotherly they, hand in hand,
  Enchanted by the magic wand,
Press onward to their heavenly goal
  And win the prize of peace.

Harmony of the universe,
Thou wast its mother and its nurse.
  Profound thou didst inspire
The mystic dance trod by the spheres
  In honor to their sire.
Their orbits, various as their years,
  Form strings to heaven's living lyre;
In joyful concert thus they move,
Forever chanting "God is love."

Friend of helpless infancy,
Our earliest vows are due to thee;
Babes owe thee their first lisping lay;
Because thou art the mother's stay
When, dreading the untimely blight,
She watcheth through the livelong night
Her drooping infant, at whose feeblest cries
Her heart is rent with sympathetic sighs.

Now with soft slumber's chain 'tis bound,
  Captive to larger freedom led;
It scarcely breathes, but sleeps as sound
  As if the gentle soul had fled.
Death oft in that disguise is found.
  " 'Tis strange. Oh, no, my child's not dead;
We must not and we will not part!"
She clasps it wildly to her heart
And strives to break the envious chain,
And yearns to catch its breath again.
In vain, alas! 'tis all in vain;

For that strong chain she cannot break,
From that sound sleep it cannot wake;
Conviction's chill doth o'er her creep:
It is—it is death's chain—death's sleep.

But love outlives the lost one's tomb
Its dismal precincts to illume,
And half dispels the horrid gloom,
   Undamped by its foul breath.
Not Lethe's flood can drown the flame,
It laughs to scorn his magic name;
In calm or storm 'tis still the same,
   For "love is strong as death."

But oh, " when youth and beauty meet,"
And eyes congenial mutual greet
Each other for the first, and seem
To know each other well, and deem
   That they have long been friends,
Say, is it but a dream
   That heated fancy sends?

Nay, Heaven's mysterious wisdom finds
Unsought such boon for docile minds,
And though it far surpass their dreams,
Their joy is all it sweetly seems.
Even as the bird perceives its mate,
   And will not own another,
They fondly think that happy fate
   Made them to be together.

Smiles he? Her cheeks with gladness glow.
Or looks he downcast? Tears congenial flow.
She loves his likings, what he blames forswears,
Adopting even his foibles unawares.
The partial mirror of each changing mood
Reflects his life, each feature more imbued.

Oh, Poesy, resign the task,
Thou canst not wear the lover's mask.
In every tongue the theme thou'st tried,
O'er every land the strain has died

That strove the tender tale to unfold,
Yet left it more than half untold.
For every happy, new-met pair
  Bid thee the pleasing theme prolong
  And consummate the unfinished song.
Exhaustless as the freeborn air,
The choirs of heaven the task must share;
  To them the pleasing task doth most belong.

See the group of sister graces,
Clasped in each other's fond embraces,
Smiling in each other's faces.
Faith and Hope the thread entwine
Of human destiny Divine,
But, Charity, the clew is thine.

Faith is our shepherdess, fair guide;
With her we climb the mountain side
  Where fruits of virtue grow.
And mounted now on Pisgah's height,

See promised Canaan, our birthright,
Where milk and honey flow.

When nightly gathered to her fold,
Each straggler sought, the number told,
Secure she bids us sleep.
Though thieves around your shelter stalk,
And pestilence in darkness walk,
Believe, and I will keep.

And pious vestal, brighter hope,
E'en in the bosom of despair
A constant vigil thou dost hold,
Lest life's Promethean fire grow cold;
Still promising a sky more fair
Beyond the clouds through which we grope.
Come dwell with me, thrice-welcome guest,
And bring thy sovereign balm;
Bind up the heart that grief hath riven,
Pronounce the wanderer's sins forgiven,

The troubled waters calm.
Physician of the soul, thy means are blest.

But, sweetest virgin of the group,
    To thee the palm be given;
More fair than Faith, more bright than Hope,
    Love, thou alone art heaven!

XVII

HOPE DEFERRED.

PRAY on, pray on, God sleepeth not,
Though His ear seem dull, and our cause forgot.
'Tis the trial of faith; oh, doubt it not!
For it worketh patience to bless our lot
    In days to come.

Hope on, hope on, though hope be delayed,
And with sickness of heart our hopes be repaid.
Still cherish the bud 'neath adversity's shade,
For the later to bloom will be last to fade
    In days to come.

Love on, love on, nor impatient complain
That love gropes in darkness and labors in pain.
'Tis the hour before dawn of charity's reign,
Who seeks not her own, but shall all things gain
        In days to come.

XVIII.

WEDDING ANNIVERSARY.

WELCOME, returning bridal day,
Thy memory knows no decay.
Each year confirms our plighted truth
With promise of perpetual youth.

Love grows not old; its daily cares
Reveal new graces unawares;
While added joys increase the store
Laid up in heaven for evermore.

XIX

LOVE BIDES ITS TIME.

KEEP the secret well concealed;
  Tell it not by conscious word:
Love can wait till time-revealed,

'Till betrayed by patient eyes,
  'Till from tender tone inferred,
Or from act in artless guise.

Gentle influence love will bring,
  Like the incense-laden breeze,
Balmy breath of budding spring,

Bearing joys we know not whence;
  Calm content and trustful ease,
Satisfying soul and sense.

Not by passion's hungry fires,
  Nor by raptures love e'er lives:
Higher motive love requires.

Love's concern for self is small.
  Love, unasking, freely gives;
But in giving gaineth all.

XX

LOVE'S SILENT INFLUENCE.

Love tells its story with the eye.
　How well the tale is understood,
The smiles of answering eyes reply,
　And prove the silent language good.

With noiseless steps love comes and goes,
　And sweet the fragrance of its breath;
We feel its blessing soothe our woes,
　But cannot tell the words it saith.

Nor think that love will claim its fee,
　Though deep the debt its zeal may earn;
Love is a giver rich and free;
　Its bounty asks for no return.

Wherever love's fair river flows,
   Another Eden charms the sight;
Where beauty's modest buds unclose,
   Diffusing ever new delight.

The crystal waters, clear and pure,
   Whose channel is the human heart,
But circulate to cleanse and cure,
   And everlasting life impart.

Flow on, forever, stream of love;
   Thy living spring can never fail.
It wells amid the courts above,
   Its fountain is the "holy grail."

XXI

BOYHOOD'S LOVE.

My boyhood's love, I feel it still;
  It lingers like a parting knell,
Though manhood's cares the place would fill
  Where it alone was wont to dwell.
  My boyhood's love renews its spell.

Bedecked with charms, all nature smiled;
  With brightest visions fancy glowed;
The pliant heart was fain beguiled,
  And rapturous tears unbidden flowed.
  Dear boyhood's love, by heaven bestowed.

How ardently my bosom yearned
 To kindle in some kindred breast
The sacred flame in mine that burned,—
 To bless with love and thus be blessed.
 Sweet boyhood's love, thou heavenly guest.

How deep, how truthful were the vows
 That young devotion freely breathed;
For love's own chaplet bound my brows,
 Of faith and high-wrought hopes enwreathed.
 Blest boyhood's love by heaven bequeathed.

The generous throb, th' impassioned sigh,
 How prodigal their wealth to give;
At love's behest content to die,
 For love alone resolved to live.
 My boyhood's love shall life outlive.

BOYHOOD'S LOVE.

And many a tear regret hath stole,
For every joy, for every pain,
Embalmed in faithful memory's scroll.
Oh, let me be a boy again,
And boyhood's love renew its reign!

XXII

WEDDED LOVE.

THE perfect mutual love of one for one,
  Each living only in the other's life,
  The holy partnership of man and wife,
'Tis paradise, 'tis heaven on earth begun.
But is life's battle over, duty done,
  When private peace and selfish joys are rife?
  No wider field for higher human strife?
So ends the game with Eden barely won?
Nay; wedded love must burst the bounds of
      home,
  Must seek the lost sheep of the common fold,
  Must penetrate the purlieus of despair.
When it hath rescued all the souls that roam
  Forlorn the world's inhospitable wold,
  Then only love may full contentment share.

XXIII.

"IF I LOVE YOU, WHAT IS THAT TO YOU?"

THOUGH I love thee, heed not me.
  Beauty is a sacred pledge.
Prove thyself a pure trustee.

Though all love thee, be not vain,
  Claiming as thy privilege
Charms which angels dearly gain.

Though I worship in thy bower,
  'Tis not Passion's greedy flame,
Seeking whom it may devour.

'Tis the homage due to Good.
  None but One may claim that name;
He imparts to whom He would.

What He giveth His remains:
  For who makes that food his choice
Union thus with Him attains.

He divides His joy with thee.
  His the music of thy voice.
Smiles betray His witchery.

He bestows the power to please;
  Lending every winning way,
Native grace and careless ease.

Only blemishes are ours;
  Errors leading us astray;
Death and all its direful powers.

Every noble tendency,
    Every blessing worth our strife,
Faith, and Hope, and Charity,

All that cometh from above,—
    But reflections of His life,
Revelations of His love.

Gazing in another's eyes,
    Fondly seeking signs of truth,
Haply one may find the prize.

Thus His flesh and blood He gives,
    Food that feeds immortal youth.
Thus man sees His face and lives.

XXIV.

L'ENVOI.

CONSTANCY (1888).

THE sands of mortal life are running low,
　The pleasant way, so long together trod,
　Draws near its end,—the bosom of our God.
The pitcher breaks, the fountain fails to flow.
What waits us in the silent land we know;
　For while we leave the body's empty clod
　To moulder 'neath the consecrated sod,
Beyond, united still, our spirits go.
As one we drank earth's cup of bitter-sweet,
　We breathed as one its duty-laden breath,
　　And common cares revealed the mutual heart.
In Heaven one path attracts our willing feet.
　What God hath joined, not man, nor time,
　　　nor death,
　　Nor life immortal shall prevail to part.

www.ingramcontent.com/pod-product-compliance
Lightning Source LLC
Chambersburg PA
CBHW021540270326
41930CB00008B/1319